Meditating with the Angels

Meditating
with the
Angels

Text by
Sônia Café

Illustrations by
Neide Innecco

SAMUEL WEISER, INC.

York Beach, Maine

First published in 1994 by
Samuel Weiser, Inc.
P. O. Box 612
York Beach, ME 03910-0612

Library of Congress Cataloging-in-Publication Data
Café, Sônia
    [Meditando com os anjos. English]
    Meditating with the angels / by Sônia Café and Neide
        Innecco.
        p. cm.
    1. Angels—Prayer-books and devotions. I. Innecco,
        Neide.
    II. Title.
    BL477.C34   1994
    291.2'15—dc20   94-17190
                                                        CIP

ISBN 0-87728-812-7

Typeset in 11 point Palatino

Printed in Hong Kong

99 98 97 96 95
10 9 8 7 6 5 4 3 2

The paper used in this publication meets the minimum requirements of the American National Standard for Permanence of Paper for Printed Library Materials Z39.48-1984

This little book is a demonstration of deep gratitude to the Angels of God, without whom "the experience of being" would not have been possible for the women and men on Planet Earth.

Table of Contents

How to Use this Book

The purpose of this little book is to inspire you to tune in to the Angelic Kingdom and invite the Angels to participate in your life. Here they are represented by keywords or qualities that can be a source of inspiration when you are facing a question, a need to clarify some fact, action, or situation in your life, or whenever you wish to meditate on a quality that you would like to see manifested in your life.

Open the way in silence and then ask a question, or clearly visualize a situation that is asking for your care and attention. Pause again silently, this time becoming receptive and allowing your subconscious mind to align itself with your Soul. Ask for an Angel to come and help you with the inspiration or clarification that you need.

As you open the book, you will find an illustration representing an Angel and the quality that it is bringing, a short passage for reflection, and an affirmation. The Angel's presence with its keyword may be enough to expand your understanding. The short passage for reflection may lead you to perceive new angles in the situation on which you are focusing at the moment. The affirmation, whenever repeated, in addition to positive thoughts and ideas, may become an effective support in the manifestation of new qualities and attitudes in your life.

All that we need to know is already within ourselves. This little book can just be a tool to support you so that you can get in touch with your most intimate essence, having the Angels as partners and messengers of the guidance that comes from the Soul.

The Angels

The Angels are beings who live in God's presence. When we become aware of them, they may inspire us to get in touch with the spiritual essence of wholeness and not to forget our spiritual origin. The Angelic Presence also helps us to clarify our choices and the purpose of our lives.

The Angels live in dimensions that do not take part in biological processes. They relate to our material dimension as forces of stabilization and rays of luminous tranquility that radiate peace and protection. The Angelic Kingdom is always vitalizing us with renewed energies of eternal love.

At this moment on our Planet, Angels are returning to our awareness to help dissolve the crystallized concepts that have blocked us from getting in touch with the source of perennial wisdom within. Their most important gift to humanity is to inspire us to change the course of our interests from fearful thoughts and actions, toward attitudes and thoughts totally centered in love. And this love is being channeled through all human beings if their consciousness is open to live with the Angels. This inner partnership will become more and more natural and synchronistic as we work with our Angels.

The Angels communicate directly with our hearts and with the innate capacity we have of being in tune with each present moment of our lives.

We are not interested in changing minds. Minds have always followed the passion of the heart. We are interested in opening hearts.

—Ken Carey
Starseed, the Third Millennium

The Angel of Patience

My patience creates miracles in my life.

With the quality of patience we will know how to follow the energy flow toward the success of our accomplishments, moment by moment, step by step. If we allow a loving patience to come through, without expecting things to happen rapidly, we will become aware that everything we do has a real value. Nature gives us the greatest example of loving patience through the wonderful treasures that it creates.

The Angel of Power

*Infinite Power, heal me! In my real beingness
I am strong, happy, and peaceful.*

Our Soul's power is revealed to the personality as a clear purpose and the capacity to decide for the good of everyone involved in a situation. Soul power is never
over someone or something. It is a power
shared with all involved. That means a
sharing of spiritual blessings that emerge
when we tune in to the divine purpose of
our lives.

The Angel of Expectation

I am always expecting the best of myself.

To what do you want to give birth? The essence of expectation is to know how to wait for that which is already conceived within yourself. It is like a pregnant woman who nourishes and cares while she wisely waits till the baby is ready to be born. Then she joyfully welcomes it.

The Angel of Education

*I am open to the education that is inspired
by my Soul.*

True knowledge comes to us when we tune
in to the Soul. All that we receive from the
external world is second-hand information.
Direct knowledge is something we can con-
tact when we realize it is already within
ourselves. Education is allowing the Soul's
latent wisdom to manifest itself, teaching
us how to live.

The Angel of Transformation

I am aware of the divine energy that moves my being and transforms me into who I truly am.

Transformation is a mysterious process that includes many changes in itself—the caterpillar that becomes a butterfly, the cream transformed into butter, the lead of heavy vibrations into the gold of the Soul. From one level to another an inner alchemy is processed and suddenly we are transformed into a new dimension. Transformation happens naturally as we surrender to the flow of divine energies that gives life to all there is.

The Angel of Clarity

*The clarity of my Soul flows through me
when I think, feel, and act in the world.*

The more we tune in to the inner light that
comes to guide our actions safely, the simpler life becomes. This is clarity, a kind of
inner knowing that leads us easily and
lightly to what is right.

The Angel of Freedom

*My Soul's loving energy flows
through my being. I am free.*

A great freedom is felt when we release the tension created by the lower centers of consciousness that trap us in attachments of power over others, money, and sensation. When we simply allow the energies of the Soul to direct our lives, we understand the freedom of being constructive and positive, accepting people and situations as they are, here and now, free from the side effects of negative reactions.

The Angel of Spontaneity

*I choose to be spontaneous in my
interactions with life.*

When we free ourselves from limiting beliefs and values, the spiritual energy flows
through us naturally. Without the inhibi-
tions that imprison our minds and hearts,
we develop an ability to tune in to the essence within people and things and dissi-
pate the fear and emotions that block us
from being spontaneous. The precision of
spontaneity is something present in Nature
and flows as a gift of love.

The Angel of Order

My outer life reflects my inner order.

Awareness of order is active on every level of creation. No being or thing would exist if processes of order and ritual were forgotten. The Sun, the Moon, the stars, and all of Nature respond with order and beauty to the Creator. When there is order, the higher energies flow without hindrance; we feel a great freedom and we don't need to worry about what to do next.

The Angel of Positivity

*My mind is filled with positive thoughts
that nourish and heal my life.*

This positivity is not something simply opposing negativity; it brings transformation and creates clear vision and right action. To be positive is to know that the energy follows what we think and feel. If, here and now, we choose to create the most appropriate and beautiful reality, the energy will respond. The light of positivity goes through the tiniest crack in our awareness and soon reveals a way for the good of the whole.

The Angel of Joy

*I feel the radiance of joy through my
whole being. I feel the joy of being
who I am, here and now.*

Angels fly because they cannot be pulled
down by the gravity of a self-imposed
gloominess. Joy is light, luminous; it comes
without creating attachment or division. Let
us be like the Joy as it flies and we will be
winged like the Angels.

The Angel of Flexibility

I am ready for the surprises of life.

When we are in tune with our Souls, we get the inspiration that will help us not to harden or crystallize in relation to our thoughts, concepts, habit patterns, or conditionings. When we are able to follow the flow of intelligent energy in the daily affairs of our lives with flexibility, we create an openness for the Spirit within us to come and make our burden light.

The Angel of Trust

The light of my Soul is my solid foundation of trust.

When we trust our inner potential, we never waste energy. Whenever we are motivated by the deepest truth within ourselves and not by others' expectations we will be giving the living example of trust. The more we allow the light of the Soul to flow through us, the stronger the foundations of trust will be to support our actions in life.

The Angel of Health

*My whole being is healthy and filled
with the energy of Love.*

The source of true health is our Inner Divinity. The loving energy that nourishes our being is always available to heal any deviation or forgetfulness that would result in sickness or disease. Visualize now any area of your body or of your life that needs to be healed. See it being showered with the healing, transforming light of Love.

The Angel of Surrender

I surrender joyfully to God's Love in my heart.

When we surrender to our Soul's guidance, we realize the greater picture of our lives. We also become aware of the help we receive to be free from burdens of the past, or from negative energies that prevent us from seeing our inner strength and beauty. When we consciously surrender to the Soul within, we can easily forego all else with simplicity and whenever necessary.

The Angel of Enthusiasm

My whole being is radiant with enthusiasm.

Enthusiasm is a burst of inspiration that comes from God. It is the certainty that we will never meet an uninteresting person or live moments of boredom. When we allow ourselves to really live this certainty, we discover the tremendous energy that is always available to us and always supportive of every circumstance in our lives.

The Angel of Birth

*I am being born each moment to
the newness in my life.*

When a cycle is complete, it holds within it
the time to welcome birth. Birth is the moment of transition that precedes a great rev-
elation. All that has just been born is full of
freshness, novelty, and innocence. Nothing
is more important than the birth of Love in
our hearts.

The Angel of Integrity

*In the integrity of my being I experience
and express the dance of life.*

The dance of polarities is a constant in our
lives: to give and to receive, to laugh and
cry, "to be or not to be," positive and negative. In that way we each carry within a
colorful spectrum of energies. Accepting
and expressing those aspects, as they are,
is to live with conscious integrity, which
means that we are channels for the living
expression of our Unified Spirit.

The Angel of Perfection

In my Real Self, life is eternal,
wisdom is infinite, love is abundant,
and beauty is perfection.

All that is complete and whole is perfect. The white dove does not need to wash for whiteness, neither does the flower in the fields beg for fragrance. The more natural and spontaneous the gesture, the closer to perfection. To overemphasize the need for perfection may push away the possibility to channel the perfection of who we really are in every moment of our lives.

19

The Angel of Blessing

I am blessed in many ways and
I bless all that I have.

To be aware and open to our true Selves is the greatest blessing. When we are blessed all those around us participate in it. Blessings never come just for one. Bless and hold sacred all that you are just now.

The Angel of Partnership

*Each one I meet is my partner
in the here-now of life.*

When there is partnership, there is no domination. The parts involved in a same situation share their abilities and talents to create a shared goal. To walk together toward that goal, aware of the process it implies, is true partnership—opposites discovering that they are absolutely complementary.

The Angel of Wisdom

Through my connection with Infinite Wisdom all becomes possible.

All that exists flows from the source of Divine Wisdom. Wisdom emerges in the heart that has opened itself. We transform attachments and doubts into the certainty that we have and know all we need when we tune in to the Soul. It is possible to have knowledge and no wisdom. Wisdom is a pure quality that comes from the Spirit, inspiring loving attitudes and creating abundance moment by moment.

The Angel of Tenderness

I am radiant with tenderness.

Tenderness—the soft breeze on the meadow, an opening bud, a hand that finds the perfect gesture, the touch that heals, the gaze of pure understanding with no strings attached. In our lives tenderness is the natural flow of our actions because the Soul has dissolved all fear of being.

The Angel of Communication

*I express clearly the voice and
wisdom of my heart.*

When we meet someone and connect with
his or her inner light, we allow the most
wonderful communication to happen, be it
with words, gestures, with a smile or even
in silence. Communication inspired by the
Soul radiates interaction and synchronicity
in our lives.

The Angel of Synthesis

*In the white light of my Soul I see
the synthesis of who I am.*

Synthesis is a key quality for understanding what the future brings. The energy of appreciation is very important in order to understand the meaning of synthesis in our lives without becoming victims of what happens. With the quality of synthesis, we develop the ability to see unity in diversity and we open the way to the inner wisdom that brings wonderful synchronicity into our lives.

The Angel of Strength

*My strength is a precious gift from my
Soul in which I am always safe.*

A great strength emerges in our lives when
we recognize that security and happiness
are Soul qualities. Our strength lies in allowing those qualities to flow through us
bringing the ability to go ahead with deep
inner security.

The Angel of Love

The more I learn to love myself,
the more I know how to love others.

"Love your neighbor as yourself." When
the healing power of Love flows through
our lives it transforms old habit patterns
and beliefs and at the same time it protects
us and lifts the energies of all around us.
Love is the reason behind all there is.

The Angel of Peace

I am infinite peace.

Peace is an inner agreement with the Soul's steady serenity. It brings a feeling that inspires harmlessness toward every living creature of God's Universe. True peace transcends our human understanding and attunes every living being with the universal harmony. The more we attune to peace, the more radiant our lives become.

The Angel of Light

*The divine light of my Soul flows
through my being right now.*

If we are in a dark room, we won't be able
to push darkness away with our hands or
with our minds. We need to turn on the
light. If we open ourselves to the inner light
of the Soul, it will transmute all darkness.
Visualize now in your heart an expanding
golden light that radiates warmth and clarity to all around you. Feel this light expanding from an inner center and becoming a radiant sun of understanding love.

The Angel of Purpose

I cooperate joyfully with the purpose of my life.

When we have a purpose, our Soul's work is accomplished in the best way possible through our bodies and personalities. A clear purpose gives no room for doubt because we identify immediately with all that leads us toward our goal. We become aware of all that would turn us away from it. The flow of energies in our lives is immense when a clear purpose is always present. Do you know what is your purpose in life?

The Angel of Responsibility

*My ability to respond makes me feel account-
able. I am joyfully responsible for my life.*

Whenever we use our ability to respond
with our talents and capacities, to all that
is ascribed to us, we are being responsible.
This can mean using those talents and abilities for the good of all in a light and joyful
way. Responsibility is only a burden when
we forget to use our talents and cut ourselves off from the flow of spiritual energies that are always waiting to help us
whenever we can respond.

The Angel of Healing

*I am a channel for the healing
energies of the Universe.*

The real source of healing is the "Inner Sun"
that radiates through our bodies with its
qualities of love and synthesis, uplifting our
vibrations and cleansing the environment
around us. True healing is to know that
we are One with God.

The Angel of Compassion

You and I are One.

When we are compassionate, we are able to understand others from deep within ourselves. This attitude brings a light that reveals truth and the love that transforms and heals. To be compassionate is to be equal, one with another, as with oneself.

The Angel of Release

My life is perfect here and now.

Our greatest release is to free ourselves from attachments of the past and concerns with the future—to be able to live in the present moment. When we do this, we concentrate our energies, and we don't lose vitality by criticizing, comparing, and judging. The quality of release frees us from guilt which is a great waste of energy. Release brings freedom from attachment to possessions or fear of loss.

The Angel of Inspiration

I feel radiant with inspiration.

Inspiration is like a shower of beauty and grace that uplifts our vibrations in daily living. It allows us to discover happiness and joy in all we do. This happens when we open our hearts and minds to the wonderful flow of spiritual energies that guides us an opens a way in our consciousness.

The Angel of Purification

*I bathe myself in the light of
my Soul every day.*

When we open our hearts and minds to
our "Inner Sun," we are fully purified by
the radiance of its loving light. All that
keeps the memory of negativity is cleansed,
and in that way we purify both mind and
body. Visualize now the light of your Soul
filling your entire being and purifying every cell and atom as it radiates to everything around you.

The Angel of Union

*I am a channel for the expression of
union among all beings.*

At the Soul's center we know a feeling of
perfect union that inspires compassion and
empathy toward all beings. The power of
union removes barriers and dissolves in-
difference. When two or more people are
united in the name of Love and Truth, there
is an overflowing of spiritual energies that
fulfills everyone with their gifts.

The Angel of Simplicity

*My life is fulfilled in the
simplicity of my attitudes.*

The more we attune to our Soul's love and
intuition, the simpler life becomes. On a
personality level, we tend to complicate
things tremendously, but when we become
receptive to our inner guidance, life becomes simple and clear, and is free from
that which is superfluous.

The Angel of Delight

I feel wonderful! To live is my delight.

It is important to know how to relate with pleasure, which has a certain ability to bring light into everything—meeting people, being with Nature, the fidelity of a loving pet, being with oneself. Delight is a pleasure that comes from within and relates with what is external in our lives in a way that makes everything more luminous.

The Angel of Beauty

I see beauty in the mirror of life.

All of Nature is beautiful and through its order and rhythm we know the truth of its laws. To feel the rhythm, to notice the sacred order in our lives is to see the beauty in a grain of sand or behind the most challenging appearance.

The Angel of Sharing

*In my temple of silence all is added to
me as I commune with my Soul.*

Sharing is a sacred moment. To give and
receive becomes the most intimate communication between two or more beings. Who-
ever communes participates in the One
Spirit of Life.

The Angel of Human Unity

*I always learn valuable things
from everyone I meet.*

To become aware of the human unity that
we can create—and of the loving support
that we can give each other—is the core of
real sisterhood and brotherhood. As we lovingly begin to accept people and things as
they are, we open a way for unity and harmony to be wonderfully synchronized,
bringing the best situations for us and everyone around.

The Angel of Grace

*Each moment is an opportunity
to reveal a miracle.*

Grace is a wonderful quality of the Spirit.
When it is manifested in our lives, it brings
the energy that uplifts our vibrations and
clears the inner barriers. To be in a state of
grace is to put into practice the certainty
that if we knock the door will be opened,
and if we ask it will be given unto us.

The Angel of Honesty

*When I am honest with myself I feel the
security and the support of my Soul
in my mind and heart.*

The first step is to be honest with yourself
and that means to be free. From the very
beginning, in any situation, if you choose
clarity and honesty, everybody will feel at
ease with the truth and will bring congru-
ence to your feelings and actions. No fur-
ther clarification is necessary, and all flows
with beauty and dynamism.

The Angel of Courage

My heart is open and full of courage.

Courage—an action that springs from the heart. All action inspired by a center of true love brings with itself security and firmness that cannot be disturbed. To be courageous is to know that fear offers no resistance to Love.

The Angel of Truth

"I am the Way, the Truth and the Life."
(John: 14:6)

All that is real is anchored in truth. Ten people can look at the same thing and see it from different angles. We are beings whose truth is anchored in the purest flow of divine energy; the more we allow this energy to vitalize us, the more the truth of our lives is manifested.

The Angel of Faith

*I have an unshakable faith in the
inner power of my Soul.*

Faith is revealed whenever we open ourselves to our Soul's Love and Wisdom. This
openness brings with it a certainty that
heals any doubt or hesitation. When we
walk in faith, the universe gives us the support we need, and we discover an inner
strength that removes barriers and allows
light to come through.

The Angel of Creativity

*The creative power of the Universe
is flowing through me now.*

We build anew when we open our hearts
and minds to the power of the Soul and
consciously allow the creative energy to
express itself through us. In that way we
learn that the creative power of the Universe is within ourselves, and we can create our own reality with our thoughts, feelings, and positive attitudes.

The Angel of Willingness

*I am happy! My actions are being
orchestrated by my Soul.*

Willingness is the ability to use our will
with love and wisdom. Love turns our
action into a voluntary one through the
heart and we begin to love what we do.
Wisdom shows the direction through clear
vision. In that way willingness brings total
happiness.

The Angel of Humor

*People constantly appreciate my
wonderful sense of humor.*

It is impossible to have a depressing
thought when we are willing to sincerely
laugh. Laughter can help us to look at our
lives from a new and stimulating perspective. So many times we live too seriously
and cause ourselves (and others) unneces-
sary pain and suffering. Humor makes
things flow, melts the ice and reveals true
beauty for everyone. Laugh! It's good for
body and Soul.

The Angel of Serenity

Serenity is part of my life. I live with serenity each moment that life brings.

Serenity brings a natural flow to every circumstance and moment, and inspires us to relate and savor everything, knowing that nothing is permanent. This serenity comes from the Soul, that steady center that nourishes us and helps us understand that the good and the bad moments of life do not last and are part of our spiritual growth.

The Angel of Understanding

*I understand all and everything because
I exercise the understanding of myself.*

When we understand who we really are, a
full transformation happens in our lives.
In the luminosity of the Soul we understand that true knowledge comes from
within ourselves and is transformed into
the real experience of learning.

The Angel of Group Consciousness

*I trust and act according to my
Soul's guidance every day.*

Soul's consciousness is all embracing and
is a strong connection within groups. In the
Soul dimension we are not separate enti-
ties and we are fully aware of our service
to humanity and to the Planet. To have
group consciousness is to respond to the
guidance that comes from the Soul and to
be synchronized in the right place with the
right people and action.

The Angel of Adventure

*Everything in my life leads me to
be nearer to God.*

When adventure comes, it is an invitation
to open the way to what is new. Adventur-
ing is a kind of permission we give ourselves to cross the frontier between the
known and the unknown. Soul-size adventure is a journey toward priceless treasures.

The Angel of Care

*I am filled with joy as I care for people
and things and all of Nature.*

Loving care is the Soul touch of light in
everything we do. Beyond a consciousness
of order and balance, when we care for all
with which we have been entrusted, there
is also an attraction of invisible helpers that
begin to cooperate with the success of what
we are creating.

The Angel of Forgiveness

I forgive myself, I forgive everyone;
forgiveness is my freedom.

A powerful feeling of freedom emerges
when we open our hearts to forgiveness.
Forgiving ourselves is the first step to forgiving others. We can learn to accept ourselves and others as we really are at present.
The greatest power of healing is in forgiving; with the Soul's help we can forgive
anyone who has hurt us. Forgiveness
teaches us about the great law of Cause and
Effect and opens our minds to divine mercy.

The Angel of Abundance

*I am Life Abundant and the
Love of God lives in me.*

To lovingly accept people and situations,
knowing that here and now all is in the
right place and in the right moment, is to
be aware of abundance. Abundance is not
a great quantity of things, but the awareness of "quality" within all we have.

The Angel of Obedience

I follow my Soul's guidance day by day.

The only true obedience is to the Soul. From that dimension within our own being come all signals, guidance, and intuition to be obeyed. When we obey in that way with all our senses, we are serving the Soul.

The Angel of Gratitude

*I give thanks and appreciate each
conscious moment of my life.*

It is very important to feel gratitude for all
that we have been able to accomplish.
When we look at who we really are here
and now, we open to the wonderful source
of spiritual energy that eternally flows in
our lives. The feeling of gratitude fills our
hearts and uplifts the vibrations of all that
is around us.

The Angel of Cooperation

Cooperation is part of my daily living.

Cooperation is the true healing for isolation. It is impossible to remain isolated when our talents and abilities are serving the joy of working together for a common goal.

The Angel of Balance

*I trust my inner balance and I
allow changes to happen.*

When the personality and Soul work together, there is a balanced flow of energies
through our bodies, feelings, and thoughts.
Through this feeling of inner balance we
free ourselves from limitations and allow
changes to happen.

The Angel of Harmony

*I am living in harmony with universal
laws; I am creating harmony at
each moment of my life.*

To be in harmony with the Universe is to
live in tune with joy, love, and spiritual
power. As we learn to live in tune with the
universal laws, we realize that we are an
inextricable part of Nature. People who live
together in total support of each other open
the way so Angels' spiritual energies can
flow in their lives and bring harmony.

The Angel of Kindness

*I am a free and powerful source
of life and kindness.*

The essence of kindness is to realize the
intricate and delicate network that we form
with the beings in every kingdom, in all
dimensions. The kindness of the Soul inspires us to care lovingly and responsibly
for our relationships with people, animals,
plants, and things. To be kind is to realize,
within our hearts, our total interdepen-
dence, and to be thankful for all kingdoms
of life, exactly as they are.

The Angel of Openness

*My heart and mind are open to
the light and love of my Soul.*

When our consciousness is open to the love
and light of the Soul, our lives gain a new
perspective. The light illuminates all that
may be still obscure and doubtful in our
minds. The presence of Love dissolves fear
and protects us, and at the same time it
radiates to everyone around us.

The Celestial Hierarchy

There is an Angelic Hierarchy composed of nine ranks of Celestial Beings that are named as follows:

1	-	Seraphim
2	-	Cherubim
3	-	Thrones
4	-	Dominions
5	-	Virtues
6	-	Powers
7	-	Principalities
8	-	Archangels
9	-	Angels

Angels in the Celestial Hierarchy

According to the Kabbalah the Angels are named as follows:

1	-	Metatron
2	-	Ratziel
3	-	Tzaphkiel
4	-	Tzedekiel
5	-	Kamael
6	-	Michael
7	-	Uriel
8	-	Raphael
9	-	Gabriel

Angel Words

The Angels are also called "Great Beings of the Music of the Word," and for that reason some words are associated with their names:

METATRON: Purpose, Silence, Truth, Love, Radiation

RATZIEL: Wisdom, Oneness, Unity, Surrender, Purification, Inclusiveness, Synthesis

TZAPHKIEL: Understanding, Clarity, Trust, Flexibility

TZEDEKIEL: Mercy, Compassion, Abundance, Humility, Right Action

KAMAEL: Justice, Discernment, Transformation, Rebirth, Redemption

MICHAEL: Beauty, Harmony, Patience, Faith, Balance, Hope

URIEL: Victory, Strength, Adventure, Detachment, Mission, Ressurrection

RAPHAEL: Splendor, Glory, Peace, Forgiveness, Brother/Sisterhood, Charity, Healing, Sacrifice

GABRIEL: Joy, Education, Communication, Grace

Angels and Days of the Week

Sunday   -   Michael

Monday   -   Gabriel

Tuesday   -   Kamael

Wednesday   -   Raphael

Thursday   -   Sachiel

Friday   -   Haniel

Saturday   -   Cassiel

Angels
and the Twelve Zodiac Signs

Aries	-	Machidiel
Taurus	-	Asmodel
Gemini	-	Ambriel
Cancer	-	Muriel
Leo	-	Verchiel
Virgo	-	Hamaliel
Libra	-	Uriel
Scorpio	-	Barbiel
Sagittarius	-	Adnachiel
Capricorn	-	Haniel
Aquarius	-	Gabriel
Pisces	-	Barchiel

Angel Colors

Metatron	-	White
Ratziel	-	Gray
Tzaphkiel	-	Black
Tzedekiel	-	Blue
Kamael	-	Red
Michael	-	Yellow
Uriel	-	Green
Raphael	-	Orange
Gabriel	-	Violet

Prayer to the Great Archangels

Ye hosts angelic by the high archangels
   led,
Heavenly powers Beneficent
Mighty in the Music of the Word,
Great ones entrusted with the sovereignty
Of infinite celestial spheres
Marshalling the Cherubim and the flaming
   Seraphim,
Ye O Michael, Prince of Heaven
And Gabriel by whom the word is given,
Uriel, great archangel of the Earth,
Raphael of healing ministry to those who
   yet in bondage are,
Guide our footsteps as we journey onward
Into the light eternal.

—Eusebius, A.D. 200

Index of Angels

Index of Angels

Index of Angels

Index of Angels

Index of Angels

Index of Angels

Index of Angels

U

Understanding, 52
Union, 37
Unity, 42
Uriel, 66, 68, 70, 71

V

Verchiel, 70

W

Willingness, 49
Wisdom, 22